Mostly
Welsh

The past is always present

Mostly Welsh

Poetry of landscape, love and loss

CHRIS ARMSTRONG

First impression: 2019
© Chris Armstrong & Y Lolfa Cyf., 2019

Cover design: Y Lolfa
Cover image: Chris Armstrong

ISBN: 978 1 78461 718 9

Published and printed in Wales
on paper from well-maintained forests by
Y Lolfa Cyf., Talybont, Ceredigion SY24 5HE
e-mail ylolfa@ylolfa.com
website www.ylolfa.com
tel 01970 832 304
fax 832 782

With thanks to

Ray Lonsdale, Ffrangcon Lewis and Robin Young for their support
and encouragement; also to the poetry website, Write Out Loud[1],
where many of these poems have previously been published.

[1] https://www.writeoutloud.net/

For Kathy

Cymric

Nant Lluest-Fach

Walking, I discover
Hills I never knew in thirty years of passing;
Valleys, deserted, hidden in folds and time:
Mair says once there was a community here
Self-contained, sufficient unto itself

Walking, I find
Landscapes we could have seen before, perhaps shared
Their riches, dreamed their past, known their present:
I'm told these Druid hills sing history itself
Sing within; only to those who hear

Walking, I find
Close by, a land cloaked in winter mists, gossamered in summer dews,
Beauty that seeks no knowing, asks no eye:
A few steps and civilisation fades beneath
Horizoned hills, and hills, and hills

Walking, I discover
A new selfdom within the old; a sole soul that still rejoices
Pure peace that comes unasked, unstrained:
Cymric vales, mystic mounds, silent tops:
Calm, cerebral lands; cynghanedd of the heart.

I, Ffynnon Di-rewi of Mynydd Bach

From the mountain
I pour forth
I give you my waters
      to drink
      and the many words
          of my waters
         to hear

My waters have seen
the gathering
on the hill
above the lake
My waters have heard
the prayers
on the grass bank
My waters have known
the worship
in the summer sun
and in the rain

I have heard the ministers
      preach
I have heard the families
I have heard the children
I have heard the gathering
      the voices raised
      in praise

From deep within
From the spirit of the hill
From the ancient land itself
I gave my blessing

Cors Caron

High above in purple-black hills
Llyn Teifi still feeds my pools
        with the same black waters
        that my mosses first knew
        before you sought me out.
Her cold waters flow through
and seep by stream, ditch and gulley
to fill each distant corner
beneath my surface sedge.

The old ruined Abbey church
in the Valley of the Flowers
        is not far distant –
        those dark waters of
        Llyn Teifi blessed it too.
Its white-robed monks once knew
my secret ways and hidden riches –
my healing herb or briar
and the purifying moss.

Many monks and men pass through:
my paths have guided the wise
        but are lost to those
        who are not schooled
        in my signs and lore.

Some still rest below:
my mires and moors hold
the history of a dozen centuries
and the secrets of many.

Could you but plumb my depths
Discover my histories and my secrets
       what stories could you tell,
       of what lies beneath
       in my darkest pools?
Poet! Your verse would flow chill and dark
as Teifi's waters before my marshes
calm their flow; what would you rhyme
with death, robbery or plunder?

Mostly Welsh

I grew up in Wales
Around the Swansea docks
I walked beneath huge cargo ships
Held up with props and blocks

I was made in Wales
Around the southern ports
I watched the big ships dock
My family guessed my thoughts

I was mined in Wales
Near valleys black with slag
And closing pits and picket lines
With many a mine lodge flag

I was forged in Wales
Watching across the bay
The glow from hellish fires
Roll steel night and day

I was taught in Wales
In Swansea's English Grammar
But little learned of little taught
And left in search of glamour

I had grown in Wales
But sailed off to sea
On ships I'd stood beneath
Dreaming beyond the quay

I have lived in Wales
Nearly all my years
It's made me what I am
A poet before my peers

I have lived in Wales
Nearly all my years
Its country, myth and culture
Hold both my heart and fears

Aberystwyth Scenes, 1970

It was always The Cabin
before her lectures
>coffee
>and Flic demolishing
>>*The Times* crossword,
>>sharing the clues but
>>writing the answers
>>as she read, smoked,
>>pushed her blonde hair
>>back.
Between lectures
repeat
>without the crossword

Once
I sat at the back of a lecture theatre
in Old College
>>absorbing a little philosophy
and feeling inferior
to all the students who clearly understood
>>so much more

Darts or dominoes
>in the Prince Albert or the Talbot
Music
>in the Folk Club behind the Skinners Arms
unless there was an essay due

Ten students and sometimes I
       sharing a kitchen in Cwrt Mawr
       returning to breeze-block cells
       to study, write or sleep
Leonard Cohen echoing through the halls

But The Cabin
       was our home
coffee
and that security of
       friends and lecturers meeting
       beneath the old film posters
       behind its steamed-up windows

The Land of a Giant

Between the dark Ystwyth and the angry sea
We walked the cold stone beach
From the swirling river mouth
To the striated rocks beneath the southern cliff
Their upended strata pointing the way across Tan-y-bwlch
Beyond the town beneath its northern cliffs

A Celtic god watches and menaces
Black Lugus on Pen Dinas Maelor:
We brave his fierce storms which shade our day
As the squall waves crash to the rattle and suck
Of displaced pebbles returning to the deep
We stumble along a tideline black with sea cast seaweed
Scattered with driftwood logs and rope end flotsam
And a headless dogfish left by Cornippyn's rush –
Pecked over by gulls, its ribs and gills show faintly pink
Against the rasp grey skin and dark stones.
The horizon is darkly slate blue beneath towering cloud black
Rain slashing to the sea oft split by lightning
And as we hasten on, stones sliding beneath our feet,
Screaming gulls take off into the wind and land again protesting
The wind blows foamy sea spume across the beach
As the blue sky above begins to darken

At the foot of the cliff we hesitate and watch
The storm pass to the north over the town

Braced against the wind we begin the climb
The steep path slippery from past showers
Treacherous but for the footholds worn into it
Three-quarters of the way up there is a sheltered dip
To the seaward side – a lookout's haven
But onward to the top, some four hundred feet high –
Now, we dare look the gods of Pen Dinas in the eye
And the horn of Maelor Gawr stays silent.
South where the sky is lightening behind the storm
The coast stretches to a grey hazed peninsula on the horizon;
The rocks below the near cliff slope are black and foreboding
Untroubled by any save the gods, the waves and the birds
Yet still, the gathering weather threatens
So braving again the wrath of Lugus
And the wave thrown foam
We hurry North
To Hen Gaer

Wilderness 2001, 2021

You see
      a land wraithed in smoke and the stink of death
You feel
      man's determination dulled by desperation and
      the hollow, guilty hope that the creeping fate might end
      at a neighbour's door.
You cannot farm in the present
At least not in Wales.

The hills were silent memorials to herds brought low,
Uncropped: a tragedy of grass grown longer than memory could ever tell;
In the yards, and at the hearth, silence bears witness
To the end of all that generations have bequeathed.
It is ended; how could life – and history – be raised anew?
Leave it, leave it…
Who, but the farmer, would start again?
Even in richer English valleys life lies low,
Depressed by death and loss.
In Wales, where wealth is tenured only in the land,
There will be no rural rebirth, no future.
What point?
We have farmed our subsidies too long,
Know they will not crop again.
Stranded without heed or hope or help:
There is no present in farming
And can be no future.

Our hills are the burden left by lost Europe.
To live in Wales is to be conscious
At our dusk only of the lost causes
That our wild sky could not embrace.

Wilderness 2001

We see,
With little immediate understanding, destruction and chaos
We see
The terrible beauty and symmetry as a world collapses.
We do not hear
The screams, but only and much later agonised, half-sensible
survivors' gasping reports
We do not, *can* not comprehend,
Life's casual destruction.
We do not want to see
What single-minded bravery wrought such devastation
Or what reason (if that is indeed the word) drove them on.
We can only see,
And, through mindless, uncaring media, see and see again
Every dreadful detail – as time passes, enhanced for our greater pleasure
By tearing, cruel, invasions of some poor soul's last hopeless words.
We, distant voyeurs,
Can do nothing but watch, struggle to understand, and wonder:
What self-immolation, what expression of pain, what voice
Can salve our surviving conscience, demonstrate our greater caring;
For what else can we do, the shock has left us mute of intelligent
thought.

We pray
For understanding and comfort
For wisdom
For help for those who control our new destinies.
We weep.

ἀλκυών

O, where roams your delicate soul
Does it yet travel the seas
     gliding afar with the tern
     or is its delight in quieter waters
     in dappled river pools or streams
Is it content to rest in the cool damp shade of the willow
watching minnows play
     diving among the nymphs
     and the sacred lotus

Empty are the ways
I no longer see you
     as I walk the glades alone
When our world was young
     craving love, I was Hylas
Following where you led
     a lustrous blaze in the sun
     a beckoning
     and I was lost

Oh Atthis, I long to hold you
     to feel your soft warmth
     the touch of your lips
     our passion
Your body brings me calm

Notes

ἀλκυών: Halcyon = Alcedo (Latin)

Hylas: Youth abducted by water nymphs (Ovid)

Atthis: A beautiful young woman of Lesbos

Alcedo atthis: The river kingfisher

Microcosm 2017

They come together
        in this place outside
yet at the centre of our world.
We have asked of them
        our destiny
Have demanded nothing of them
        except our future.
Who are these gods in whom we place our trust?
Who are these gods that we have selected?
        These are the senate that we once elected:
The senators that serve a mighty ruling role.
Are these our lawgivers?
Yes, we voted!

They come together
        in this place outside
yet at the centre of our world.
And what mischief there is wrought!
        Will we never learn:
Any company drawn from our world will
        like that world contain
        a sample of all our shades?
Yet we wonder at their insufficience
        gasp in horror at malfeasance
We come to know that we are governed either
by the fallible or the foolish
For whom we voted!

They come together
      in this place outside
yet at the centre of our world.
Are we so careless
      of our guardians:
These angels that we charge
      to keep us in all our ways?
Again and again, our hopes are dashed
What higher power can ensure
      That only the good endure?
Who will guard the guards themselves?
What moral high ground can we now take
When we voted?

One People

I will not fight, I will not stand
For border, nor for any land
I need not know, am not concerned
Your place of birth or language learned
Too many wars are fought, too many die
Over province, pride, triumphal lie

I will not guard, I will not bar
The stranger landed from afar
They need a home, and wish to settle
Want to work, to show their mettle
We can only profit from their work
Whether labourer, nurse or office clerk

You should not hunker safely down
To protect and shield your hometown
Look outward and welcome all the new
Who may enrich whate'er you do
Then they may live within our sphere
And raise their lovely children here

They may never learn the native diction
This may be choice, not dereliction
You should not force your homeland view
They have their culture just like you
Let the magic of our land, our nation
Embrace their souls with jubilation

Role Reversal

¿Le gusta este jardín, que es suyo? ¡Evite que sus hijos lo destruyan!
Malcolm Lowry*

It had been a good party…

But
As more arrived, we decided we had to go –
Too quickly; or perhaps too slow
For some, who said it would be best
For most if not the rest
Uncaring of the past
Or the gloom we cast
Bickering with old friends
About the future trends
Arguing with our peers
Over their misplaced fears
We left!

Grabbing the wrong coats
And the best man's notes
Our children in a rage
That nothing would assuage
Trampling garden flowers
As if all right was ours
Slamming the gate
Behind our hate
Breaking its old latch

We shunned the patch
Refusing to talk
Or even listen
We left!

We knew
We could never return to their table now
He said 'Did you like that garden, that was ours?'
  He knew it had been a place of peace
  Where harmony might yet increase
He said 'They will never let our children in to play again'

Note

* From *Under the Volcano*, translates as: 'Do you like this garden, that is
 yours? See to it that your children do not destroy it!'

Druid Lane

We came upon
A mystic way leading nowhere but the hills.
Floored in leaves, tree roofed, bank-bound
Untrodden but by wanderers for centuries past.
What lay beyond, worthy of such industry?
Perhaps a long-forgotten hearth tenured by shepherd or crone.
Or did this tended track pass on to a hilltop way:
Miles now lost to grass and sheep,
A one-time druidic path to some time-eroded henge
The copper leaf-rustle underfoot speaks of many passings
Hidden in time.

Druid Lane (2)

Who went before, who follows?

How many ages' passage are hid beneath the leaves;
    What is the past that this way could tell:
        Of travellers and stragglers; of voyagers and the lost?

In these hills the land remembers – but we can only guess:
    The tryst, the parting;
    The camp, the lone smoke drift.
    The way to market, homestead, chapel;
    Destiny: the hilltop, or the flock.
They travelled east – perhaps with tarfoot geese to distant mart
Or west, homeward bound from distant travels on far-off shores.
Did the older footfall of a Roman legion first press the road
Whose clay still knows their sandal step? Or was it the lighter tread
Of a nomad tribe, skin clad and wary of each new crested rise,
That shaped a way?
The ghosts of brigand, cleric, farmer, squire and page
People the road
    But only the ancient beeches see them pass.

Pastoral

For Gwen, Anne and Eryl

In that happy heady grass-green Spring of my years
A time of lambent lamb slow lamb full days around a whited cottage
Lent us space and ease beneath the sun long sky
Golden glorious hours together in a single thought
With close chicken scrape and distant herd
When the swallows dipped to the fly buzz
When the kite climbed to a gliding speck
     And we knew peace
We knew our place in the low home mountains of the Bards
And uncaring of the wider world
Settled there amongst the poppies and the elder
Amongst the hedge rich blossom and the tall grass
In the farm heart –
Behind the red gate, shed-hidden, summer-walled
Beneath the beech trees
And down the warm, pale moon dusk
We lay beneath Owain's blessed heaven

And in those sun born, sun run, hay heavy days
When field toil was over, limbs weary from the heft and heft of it
The barley rose golden high and heat bowed in the field
Sheep speckled the distant hills while lambs capered in Rhos Ceiliog
And the cows walked home their sun warm calves
Each uncertain step proud mothered along the track
At dusk, there came to us young girls on horses
     Bidding us ride

And in the low warm sun, we raced heedless across the grass green
fields

Careless beneath the dusk blue sky
As stars assayed a first glimmer and the red setting lit the western hedge
A thundering jouncing passage to the evening star
And back to the snorting whinnying hay warm shed
Steaming horses rubbed down and fed burst bale new cut grass
Then led to the quiet field on the hill above the lake
And we were moonlit home
And lay beneath the pale summer stars in the deep blue sun warmed sky

Then, sweet was the time lit by stars in that summer dusk
The warm night hours slow darkened by a mindful moon
Outside our window and our minds the tree-bound stubble fields
The dew-damp barley head bowed before the harvest cut
And soft on the wind a distant lowing or a far lamb bleat
Is lost beneath the dipping moon and the hunting owl's flight call
Over the hedge rustle or the grass whisper of field mouse or vole
      But we are heedless
All save love is lost to us in the warm room beneath the slates
Nothing cared we that soft night
Save for the passion pressed close within our arms and love
The closer grasp the elated press and joy of the other held
The quiet journey up to the star high moon held gasp of harmony
Then tender peace amongst the soft night airs borne of the window gape
When sleep held us close Endymion lost with Selene deep beneath
the sky

To lie as early dawn
Blazed softly blue fading starlight behind the bird sung mist hung
trees and fields

A Dalliance of Kites

Last week's snow left ice wind behind, and
Above the rush and whistle through the trees
    I hear a higher mewling,
As of buzzards hunting,
But soft on the wind a pair of kites have made the
      air their own – wheeling and drifting across the sky.
Each echoing each, keeping station, faithful, clear;
      enjoying both wind and company –
        a rushing swoop and pause
           to turn as one and drift back along the wind's edge
        to catch a current and whirl from sight and circle back.
Effortless flight born of feather slant and unlearned art –
A last slanting pinion-touching swoop and in the wind's lull, up again
To their separate ways, 'She hers, he his, pursuing'

Autumn

And then, suddenly, it was calm – the morning wind which threw
rain hard against the window panes and sent beech leaves rushing
across the grass to pile gold-brown against all that the borders grew,
all slowly dulling their greens to wet, muted browns, brushing
the soil as their leaves curl and droop – vibrant Spring-strength gone,
fading sadly.

   The wind has also left yellow leaves – and larch spines –
to cover the surface of the pond. Along with plump white rowan
                   berries,
the dying leaves of the water lilies and the pondweed which entwines
daily cover the surface of the water: they are my Autumn adversaries.
The water will not stay clear for long if I am not attentive.
It will freeze soon.

     Calm, but somehow the stillness – and the late-day
slow diming light – speaks more powerfully of the coming winter's
                     tour
than did the heralding winds. It is still raining and hills, in shades of
                     grey,
are lost to cloud. Beyond the window beyond the field on the moor
are dull brown reeds and empty willows stretching to a far wood.
And a wisp of smoke.

      Despite rain, despite wind, despite the diming light
the birds stay busy at their feeders… despite each other… for each
                     perch
is keenly held. It didn't take long for all to discover the larder's
                  delight:

I am certain that when the sun lost its heat a few weeks back, in the
                                                                    birch
one bird was stationed ready – or overhead – to watch and trumpet
the news around the parish.
                    The moss-topped wall has gained ferns:
maidenhair-like their black stems glisten. There are still garden flowers
but no butterfly still seeks the buddleia's dark and dank brown panicles
nor turns to the brash orange of the montbretia – each blooming head
                                                                    now
lost to seeded spike! The lady's mantle which once held a jewel drop
in each leaf's heart damply droops.

Above the Valley

As we pass through this Autumn realm,
See the valley-bound wraiths of mist
Withdrawing like a tide from the willow
Islands of the marshland
With their starkly black boughed trees
Damply dripping with the mist's remains,
Chill air swirls in the rising breeze, and
Black starlings line the wires beyond a barn
But the red kite in his higher flight
Is lost to sight
      and only heard.

Between the valley and the heights
We cross the dampened upland ffridd
Still veiled in its grey-bright dampened air.
The heath is springy underfoot
With moss pools often hidden in the turf,
Great grass clumps rise between
As if remembering trees that once had been.
Where the land rises towards the hills
Patches of gorse and bracken surround stone ruins:
A red-berried rowan offers cheery thanks
      for its survival.

Now, the swirls of mist that hid the way
Give way to a crisply clear blue heaven above
Two red kites drifting on the still cool breeze.
Did these same watchers in our mountain skies
Watch as the hill fort or the henge was raised
Or see the slaughter of Caradog's men –
Do they still remember as they glide
What once these mosaic hillsides saw
Or is their focus only on the ground below the wing?
Do they even see us as they pass over,

      zephyr drifting?

Winter from a Window

The empty stems of the fennel
Under umbrella heads of raindrops
Are perches for the waiting birds

The grey-green sage leaves
Glow crystal white in the frost

Moss grows where the branch
Leaves the trunk of the bonsai
Its ruddy leaves falling

Amongst the yellowing leaves
A single crimson rosebud perishes

Yellow leaves have fallen from the dogwood
Leaving its blood-red stems
Amongst the tangle of a Russian vine

On the ground
Sparrows squabble

Forvie, March 2017

Dunes…
And then the sand flowed like the tide
Shifting the land at the wave edge of the sea
A vast striated plane of drifting whirling grains:
Aged dunes lost to the wail will of the wind.
As we walked close by the sea suck and ripple
The bound beach rose and swallowed our grounded feet
We seemed to be free floating dune cloud high
In the sandsmoke drifts rushing to their new horizon.
Bleached beached twigs, shells and most sea flotsam
Were lost in that gritty cumulus over which we passed,
Buried as the golden patterned drift swept endlessly by.
Alone and spectral solid in the blown sand haze,
A larger knotted eye of arm-thick rope
Interrupted the tiding sand, arresting the wave flow
To create a tiny sheltered lee shore, a curved cove,
The sand building against its woven coir cliffs and headlands.
What tiny beached survivor will seek shelter there
In vain to ride out the dreadful storming sand?
Tomorrow, only a low gold grave mound
Will mark its buried braid bound bay.

Later, we found the sand shrouded chapel,
Last sign of a fishing village
Elementally lost to
Dunes.

A Seascape and Lowry

The horizon is an eternity distant;
The waves stretch endlessly away, yet
Always thrust closer: no focus here
Save infinity

Where was he, mid-ocean with no sign of shore?
No beach, rock or pier, but low on the water
His painter's eye saw the vast sea surrounding, the bleak sky
Enclosing

Vast miles – lost between the closest ripple
And the scarce-seen world-end roller –
Scale the wonder and terror of this emptiness
Unchanging

He said, what if it suddenly changed its mind
and didn't turn the tide? And came straight on?
If it didn't stop and came on and on and on and on
Threatening

Lost Love

I am quiet now you are gone
now I am the sole sound in the night
darkness swallows my words:
those grey echoes of my brain's flight
fade with the soft shadows
in the ice-cool moonlight
shading the garden of my mind

I am quiet now you are gone
for you were the soft song of nightfall
and my sad soul's dawn light
whose coy brilliance would enthral
sundering cold dark shades
to make moon and stars thrall
to the sunlit garden of my mind

I am quiet now you are gone
for I am the silence of our dreams
darkness surrounds my mind
only a whisper of my thought seems
to drift with the night owls through
the star chilled light streams
in the barren garden of my mind

Parallel Echoes of Love

In the long small hours of dark	Through the later time of darkness
I pause and gaze out at the stars	As we lay entwined beneath the moon
Somehow the frosted ground	The nightly scene now sacred
Sharpens the air and the starlight	Welcomes the soft moonglow
Which lights my very soul:	Entering both our hearts:
Merciless piercing ivory light	Soft gentle hunting owl light
Naked, I move across the grass	Gladdened, we move across the space
Out, to the exact star centre	On and on, to our close high point
To lie, and stare at heaven	To lie, and feel our heaven
Crucified	Satisfied

Succubus

waking
in their bed
beneath the slates
waking
as in a dream
slowly aware
waking
completely
waking
in the window airs
waking
in the hush
of the night
palely lit by her lucent light
the night
calls to him
and he walks out
the night
absorbs him
summer dew wet on his feet
her cool breath on his naked flesh
the quiet mysterious night
scarcely disturbs his stillness
still lumined by the pale moon
rapt, transfigured
he seems to pass through her darkness

on, beyond, beyond the garden wall
on, to that other world of heath and fell
where plashy moss soft cushions his feet
and as the mists drift up
the night welcomes him
to her chamber
her soft airs
whisper
caress
but as the sun rises
waking
them in their dormered bed
he lies dazed
not believing
his Ysbrydnos

Note

Ysbrydnos: 'spirit night' when spirits are out and about divination is
    possible

Absalom's Rise

Were you not my watchtower, erect above the chalky cliff
Stone guardian against all, high over the rough tides of my youth?
Was yours not the bastion, planted secure on the high turf:
Whose high walls embraced us and protected?
But that was then, now I am the ascended man –
I do not see your turrets from my farther shore
Black waves broke on your defences, your mortar crumbled.
I stand alone, I do not need your agèd strength

From those same rocks that formed my cliff-top tower
Came the ore from which I was hot forged and grew.
Paired with passion's deepest fire and borne of love
Their strength shaped, their union created me.
But that was then, now I am the iron formed man,
Am I not the guardian buttress whose mighty steel
Subdues the old enemy, checks the bleak storm, deflects the barbs?
I stand alone, I no longer need your ancient stone

Now the heat of your fires is lost to ash, I do not seek your warmth
Now your walls are tumbled, they offer me no shelter –
Do I not stand as you once did, a mighty tower watching over all?
Your foundations anchored us, your brave stones gave refuge.
But that was then, now I am the central pillar raised over all
High formed battlements are set against all lineal tribes
Ramparts strongly built that no tide will scour, no word no wave destroy
You stand unseen, I need only my native strength

The Messages

What words have passed
What said
What read
What meaning cast?

What recall flows
What thought
What tort
What grievance shows?

What edge is crossed
What line
What sign
What friendship lost?

What nightmare grown
What meme
What seam
What darkness sown?

What text is read
What hyped
What typed
What despair fed?

What love has gone
What cord
What chord
What tumult drawn?

No One Hears

Though they are mine
I have no wisdom
Though they know me
They are deaf

  In their mind
I am a man apart
I am all that is left
I am the helix of their birth and death and being
   Knowing one, I know all
I am a voice
I seek nothing I seek peace
I hear all and I reflect
I see words and I grieve
I sense their pain and I weep
I feel their tears and I despair

Though they are mine
I do not bring peace
I am an empty meeting place
I am an abandoned pulpit
I am an echo of reason

I have no home
I am a sailor with no ship
I am a teacher with no college
I am a reader with no library
I am an old and naked man
I am a dreamer of dreams

Though they are mine
They hear no wisdom

Ancestral

Am I to speak for your past?
        May I?
        Should I intrude?
For I am the spectre of your years: I was there beside you
In your cot and at your play
Now
I am all that is left
        I am the breath of your childhood
        I am the oxygen of your life
        There is no limit to my presence in your life
                I am in your soul's deepest recess
                        and in each drop of blood

For I am the cleric of your past
        I intercede for you
                and I wonder:
Do our ashen dead reach out from where they drifted,
wise on their lakeside hill or in the garden plot
        to remind you of their love
        to whisper guidance
        to support
What do you remember of the words they spoke
        Or wrote:
These, your ancestors.
What memories have they bequeathed
        to haunt the dusky corners of the room

to drift like leaves across your Autumn life
or to shimmer some reflected lustre?
Do you ever think of them
from the cosmos of your world

I come to you from afar
but stop at the door
And I wonder:
Am I lost to you as they are lost to you
Is my oxygen burned to ash
Have you no need of my perfect dream
Knowing nothing beyond each small minute

For
I am all that is left
I have been everything and nothing
I remember all things; I remember nothing
I am what remains of your tender years – I am the shade of
your childhood
I am all that has passed – I am the ghost of your manhood
I am the shaman of the tribe
I am your radiant nimbus, drifting
away

Know me as you move through the world alone
Remember my eye's soft blue love and darker shadows
For too soon, before you may reach for me again
you will become all that is left
the only memory

.

Zen Reflexions

To discern
    our place
To commune
To see
    beyond our close shadow of death   i
To focus
    my poet mind
I need direction
    a qibla   ii
Or some beads to tell
    to take refuge from my life:
A candle flame
Only the candle
Flame
Flickering.
A journey into quietude
    begins
Into that silence
    comes tranquillity
And the absence of words   iii
Serenity beyond words:
    I become sentient –
    conscious of only this moment in the flame of a grain of sand iv
        Of the sun shining through golden autumn trees
        Of the clearing mists
        dissolving in the valley and above the hills

> *giving way to rain that fills the sky*
> *so that the branches droop, dripping*
> *as the wind rustles the upper boughs*
> *and drops spatter on the window glass.*
> *Of love*

Peace

Perhaps, now, I am no longer physical

But have become a spiritual being ^v

having a human experience

Writing

And in the writing

the words return

Notes

i   Molière: 'Without knowledge life is no more than a shadow of death'

ii   Spiritual direction (the direction of Mecca)

iii   Zen Master, Hung Chih, writes of serene reflection in which one forgets all words and realizes – is aware only of – Essence.

iv   *c.f.* Blake: Auguries of Innocence: 'To see a World in a Grain of Sand…'

v   'We are not human beings having a spiritual experience, but…' Generally attributed to Pierre Teilhard de Chardin, SJ, a French idealist philosopher and Jesuit priest

A Dream Itself is but a Shadow

In the grey cloudlight of a pre-dawn moon
something stayed my dream
a stray insistent sigh heard through sleep
the uncertain call of the hunting owl:
I am knelt naked at the window –
beneath, the frosted grass glimmers in the pale creamglow
hazy through the early swirls of mist
but neither shade nor waft disturbs the spectral scene
although my flesh seems chilled by some slight air.
The owls have drifted far and their calls echo off
skeletal trees standing black guardians to the scene
holding the far world at bay while dark unlit patches
shade lost and hidden secrets in the abyss below
I, visitor to this spirit world, observer
to this closer orbit, like the owls,
hunt for wraiths in the night's phantasy
seeking the whisper, the faint breath that woke me
the touch that raised the hairs on my arm
yet vanished as I called and called
my cries fading into the garden airs
as if she had never been

Notes

The title is borrowed from *Hamlet*, Act 2, Scene II

Phantasy: In psychological writing, the spelling phantasy is often used to differentiate the concept as used by Melanie Klein to represent an innate unconscious process, from the related Freudian concept fantasy, which is conscious and deliberate.

Dream, Schmeme

We were, two friends and I,
Lost in a hotel
Or perhaps it was a ruined synagogue
Or village
Or all three.
I remember two of us looking
into several rooms with beds
I sat on one. Briefly. And drank water.
And I remember quite clearly
a corridor running the building's length –
or maybe it ran through several buildings –
then another path back, outside at the rear;
and clambering over rubble into rooms –
two of us being endlessly shown around
by a bearded rabbi dressed in gabardine and fedora
who in some rooms fell to his knees and bowed in prayer
leaving us unsure whether we should follow suit:
I did, she didn't.
In one room his chanted shema was surprisingly, sonorously loud
and he pointed to a strange microphone like a broken lamp,
hung on old frayed and twisted wire from the remains of the ceiling.
When, in one room where we had climbed over a fallen beam to enter
he met a fellow rabbi entering through another door
they hugged and then prayed together.
Again, the doubt!
Finally we stumbled out of the ruin into a street

I think he stayed behind.
In the bazaar or souk
we seemed to be looking for a meal.

Suicide's Beck

To a friend

There is a small and unremarkable bridge I often cross
That now stands guardian to the memory of a friend.
When your burden became too much, it held you in its thrall
And gave passage across your own imagined Styx.
And on that very day and hour your demon choice was made
What base chance made me bypass the bridge, and you?
This is left to me: the possibility of deliverance that day;
And the knowledge that I should have heard your cry long before.
Had I passed there, do I imagine destiny would have changed its course,
Fate recast the script? Could we have pulled back from despair's brink;
Overcome the blackness and rejoined your life untouched?
Could breath have ever been the same again?

There is a small and unremarkable bridge I often cross
And in its crossing mark my loss,
      and his: he was much more than he'd believe;
Thus, I remember; thus, I grieve.

The Traveller

Alf Smith was his name, though, we should remember him
As more than labourer on a small Welsh farm
Who milked the cows and tended every farmer whim;
Twice daily fitting clusters onto teats and pouring milk to churns,
Taken for collection to stand beside the lane between the ferns.
Twice daily, too, he cleaned the shed with hose and broom
And waited to hear what chores would fill his waking hours.
His are the menial tasks: in summer sun or winter gloom
To walk to field flock or herd, check ditches, carry peat
Bring tools, load bales: not for him the tractor's seat.
For his food and roof he laboured hard and long with small return
The whitewashed sheds, the bale stacks, the tidy yards
The dairy and the cattle shed were all his chief concern
Too often there was unkind word and impatient yell
He took it all, but his complaints were muttered well.
His weathered face and kindly smile, his old suit jacket, and his cap
Greased shiny from years of leaning into stock; his self-rolled smoke
And gentle voice define this part of him that I first knew – but leaves
                                                          a gap.
Before the farm he walked the road and worked a summer week
On farms he passed along his way. No one knew – or seemed to seek
His story, except he came from Bristol where there may have been a
                                                    sister or a wife
From whom the war had distanced him, he would not say. Now he
                                                    walked the country way
To work and stay until the urge to move took hold: a traveller's life.

Sleeping under hedge or hidden in a barn when the sky was lost to
storm
Walking the same route year on year, the seasons set the form
Until he tired of travel and settled down to labour on that small
Welsh farm
That after many years of toil left him to settle in a caravan beside its yard
To pass his later years at peace with life, at last some years of resting calm
Remember him, then, for he will always be a part of this farm's past
Staid as the land, this kindly man whose life beneath the stars was vast.

From 1923

Too soon, we recognised
a fading spot at life's centre;
a glimmer
slow-darkening lineal light
        soon lost.

How should we understand our loss; or hers?
Somehow – quietly –
        she was at the family heart:
        cache to our memories, she
        heard our tales,
        told our stories.
No person or place was lost to her.

Wise in her nine decades
        she knew fulfilment's knell
            and was content –
                more so than we.
Now, I saw her ninety years in shades:
        life drawn only as
            father's daughter
            husband's wife
            children's mother –
                It had been enough!

What might have been? Lately, she had wondered…

For Brenda Armstrong, 5th January 1923 – 29th June 2015

Reminiscences

Enduring Pictures in the Mind
(Arboretum, 1970)

It was a place of trees and snow
An outing to be out
To be alone together, alone in the joy
Of first love.

Among the trees and snow,
Did we wonder at those aged limbs
Think of the years they had; and that we might
Or were we lost in love?

Among the trees and snow,
Did we feel the transience of ice
Know it would pass in so brief a span
And understand its passing message?

Cariad

Cariad
A word of the heart
Born deep in the being,
     resonant with the land's love

Cariad
A word for the soul
Harmonic with soft timbre,
     warmed on heart's ember

Cariad
A word from the deep
Breathed only in love –
     impossible to deny

Cariad
A word never of the brain
Soft spoke; heart's heat
     eased through love's light

Cariad
A word ancient as time
Nurtured well by gentle dreaming
     mists, soft as love's embrace

Cariad
Scarce heard in the ear,
Shouted loud in the brain. Thought
     overwhelmed by love's silk touch

Ocean

Restless: my body is your ocean; my limbs the currents of the sea

You float on my waves – sink only a little

I hold your sacred vessel safe – we become one:

Unite in perfect harmony

Your body runs its course through my being

I feel you cleave my waves

I know you as we sink

Black waters closing

And I know you as we rise

I hold you to float above the tide as we burst waves apart.

In the still of the calm you drift in my currents

Finding your port

Cruel Parting after Such Passion

O woman left behind!

O ship
>Of steel and rivets: deck, bridge, hull and keel:
>Fore and aft, moored tight to me
>Cargo holds: soon filled
>Cabins! One cabin I know so well!

Bearing him away

O man
>Of charts and night watches
>Scanning horizons: navigating so many seas
>Do you dream of me? Pine?
>>Touch me in your dreams?

O woman left behind
>You can only pray…
>and wait:
>>It is easier to sail away than be left home!

Mystery of Love

As we lay together
on that sun-dappled sheet:
limbs
  limp
    tangled
breath
  warm
    ragged
we knew it all
  and lost it all too soon.

As we dreamt together
in that sleep-softened bed:
bodies
  close
    safe
minds
  quiet
    dreaming
we knew our future
  but saw so short a way.

As we lived together
in that child-scattered home:
babes
  soft
    suckling

sons
      strong
            learning
we knew life's riches
      yet death held cruel sway.

The Consultant

First, the over-quiet room where we sat together
Waiting, quiet as all the others – waiting
Until she left me for the first time…
      Then I was called

As he spoke the shock hit, solid as a punch;
Left me breathless, faint, unmanned;
So obviously lost that chair and water came
And briefly the patient was I – not her.

Then my mind began to grasp the truth it had shunned;
Clarity returned with the grave timbre of his voice –
Inflected to ask: How could I not have seen or guessed
The destiny she had known so long.

How did she stand the months in which the pain was hers alone?
After all those many years, my failure to feel –
My hiding from the very possibility of that horror –
Still strikes: so hard as that first blow.

We became blind to other futures
We were one union of body, heart and soul
I lived within her and she within me: one mind, one thought,
But I did not comprehend her need, nor she mine
She left,
      and I live on knowing the chasm of that failure

Loss

In those darkest, darkling months
when both belief and hope were lost
when love was stretched taught beyond endurance
when pain and understanding spiralled
Still
There was some doubt of destiny:
      could love be snatched away;
      and child a mother lose?
A new reality must supplant all we knew
                    and dreamt.

A selfish whisp'ring worm wondered at my loss,
                not hers
           What would I never know again?

Hope

Yesterday, the sun shone black upon my soul
Depth's depth deep beneath my heart.
Lumined ne'er by hope
Thoughts sank weighted low

Today, dawn'd, in heaven's mantle rais'd
Glims golden future in my mind.
Light lightened all by future faith
Heart, mind and soul exalting up

Her voice love levered up, returned it from the depths
Dark voids where happiness was stranger.
Sweet syntax, sound, scintilla of a hope
Revives joy 'gainst something sometime void

Let not my soul's heart drear decline again
Voice defeats pen, vision understanding
I heard and saw perception peak.
Tomorrow's future lends little light today

On Leaving a Hospital Room

The sky in front of me is pink, as I drive home,
there will be a frost tonight.
Beneath it the brackened hills lie pinkly rust
And trees stand starkly laced in contrast
I see every distant twig defined, sharp against the pearlescent sky.

Not much later, I sit over tea and look west
to where the sky is left creamily gold.
Above, the darkling blue is split by a fading pink contrail;
The garden trees shift and rustle in the wind
And the horizon is lost to the closer lacework of the leafless hedge.

Unsaid, Unsung

Everything I have ever said to you
Hangs in the air between us
Not quite the reality I had in mind
Not quite

Everything I had ever wanted to say to you
Echoes only in my mind
Grieving me with its reticence
Grieving me

Every thought I have ever had about you
Lives on for ever in my memory
Saddening me with its false reality
Saddening me

Every word I have ever had from you
Read from you, heard from you
Consumed, re-read, mined for meaning
Now echoes hollow in the void
Now echoes

We should have said much more, heard more
Written more, been so much more, meant more
Too much lost to silence
Too much

Danse Macabre

Too much was lost in silence
too long the time that winds
between our words of love and passion
with communion only in our minds

Too much assumed in union
of our two souls' mute desires
but I did not see her inmost needs
or hear how quietly pain suspires

I should have peeped inside
while she nightly dreamed in peace
to glimpse her mind's apparel
as it danced its silent slow release

I should have explored her mind
when she slept in our famous bed
but selfishly I rested too
and never saw it dressed in hellish red

What should I have there espied
far below each day's loving view
those crimson twisting shrouds
half smothering the love that grew

When I once had time enough to spare
I failed to read her deepest core
to see the power of cruel invasion
reach past love to that darker shore

Passing

Time stretched as she faded;
Lengthened, folded in on time
Extended, never ended.

Eternity must have seemed
An earthly hell
Peopled intermittently by friends:
A nightmare dream of pain and daemons

What superhuman will
Kept her through those summer months
What need, desire or wish
Held death's sad end at bay?

In the end, fading faded
Light left, sylph shaded,
That faintest whispered breath sighed out
As we all knew it must.

'Gainst our hopeless hopes
She saw a means to give us strength:
Fortitude, courage, power –
But death rewards us all with death.

Two Verses from a Single Day

The Short Day

Her beauty in the morning
captured me
and I spent my life enraptured
Her beauty in that evening
was lost to me
and I felt my life collapse

Naked

We died alone in silence
We were laid bare
      for a short eternity
There were so many
Sharing our grief
She left alone
Silently

Words

words
       no man should know
       or say
words
       no child should hear:
       parent, pray
       to be spared.
As he sat with his sons at home
and struggled to find
words:
he knew
       she will never return to us
he knew
       she is too ill

In a time when she was strong
for them
as her body weakened:
he knew.

As she shrank before his eyes
skin loose on bones
flesh fading
voice whispering
       eyes sunken
       mouth dry:

no sustenance
but ice chips:
he knew.

The day she needed,
pleaded
        Help me to die
a moment of weakness:
he knew.

Alert with no strength
knowing with no words
loving with no expression
lying with no movement:
he knew.

And so he spoke the words
and died
inside:
        Your mother…
        She will never return to us
        She is too ill

Beyond Death

I find that I must live in a world
Where, between that desperate dusk and a new dawn,
And between many a dawn and its dusk,
The only reality lies in love.

To be in love in that first dawn
And in the dusk, was to feel the sun
Warm our very passion every minute of every hour,
Reality lay only in the other.

And beyond that dreadful dusk, nothing
but dawns and dusk and dawns; time, that standing still
still passes, leaving memories of so many dusks
Wherein dawn seemed no reality.

Many dawns have passed, and many dusks;
And with each new day, hope is fresh-born.
Life may once again light dawns and comfort dusks,
With some pretence of love.

In my Mind

She is so long ago.
Memory becomes mist
And past becomes perfection

She is my only memory.
Held fast in shared occasion,
While the look and touch escape

She is all my heart has left.
But can my fingers or my lips
Retain the impress of her form?

She is so long ago.
Yet daily I have her with me.
My mind holds her yet a while.

K.

Ah! I loved you!

Lost to your soul,
    I bared my heart

Within your mind
    I held my heart…

        as if all hearts sang with mine
            as if all lips knew

I felt your blood pulse
    and heat my soul
    as your hair scourged my body

        (Ah! I loved your hair!)

Mirrored in your eyes
    I felt my skin tremble

Feeling your touch
    I bared my breast…

        for you to enslave and own
            as if all flesh cleansed

I felt your dominion
    and withdrew from the world –
    as worshipping drained my soul.

Simply

Simply
Were complex not the nub of it
I need
        above all else to hold her close

Simply
If that did not deny the truth of it
I love
        and cannot imagine life without

Simply
For my love is nothing but clear crystal
I mourn
        the fading of dreamt horizons

Simply
Even when emotion crowds simple out
I know
        that love can never win

Simply
Because truth sings inescapably loud
I know
        that she is locked within me always

Love

There is no meaning
        and no sense,
        only clarity

I loved you and my heart began –
        past years unknown
        past pulse forgot

        Love created!
        Our heart defined
        our lips sang
        our hands mapped
                love

I loved you with my eyes   your eyes mirrored love
I loved you with my mouth   you sang love
I loved you with my soul   you preached love

        My being quickened:
        My dust lived in your rain,
                grew in your sun
        I clothed you with my passion

I loved you as I felt you ebb
      passion passing
      joy muting
      love defining.

And now

I love you

Still

Lost

And then

    at my source
I was lost to your ocean.

Flowing… your endless bounty stole my direction
    your depths embraced
    your corals welcomed my load
I drowned in your currents.

My hands caressed
your waves
My body plumbed
your deepest sounds
Your pools
received

Your tides were constant
    I swam in their surge
    was lost in their ebb.

And then

    your waters receding
I dried on your shore.

Memories

I remember
The long dark ache of our journey here
When I might have helped and held
And dreamt of more

I remember
Your tousled, sleep-drowned head on the pillow
When I brought you coffee;
And the pangs of love

I remember
A walk in the mists amidst the hours of work
When I should have held your hand
And talked of love

I remember
The quick shock and the long shadowed news
When all I could do was gasp and fail
And you knew my love

And I remember
The soulless, soul-destroying room where many came
When I should have held you long and tight
And never let you go

Meaning

The sound of one hand clapping
     Who said that?
But I know what it means, now:
It is the lost beat of one heart loving

Not waving but drowning
     I know that one:
Both origin and relevance now:
It is no pleasure, but one soul's need

No man is an island, entire of itself
     Sung, used, re-used
The obvious is no less
poignant now that I've found and lost my land

I am two fools I know.
     The same poet's wisdom.
My love and its focus
Both held in the duplicity of one mind's belief

We live for small horizons
     Another poet –
Another truth to learn:
We are all landlocked by the limits of our dreams

Monument

Leopardi: Such wast thou... and Ezra Pound

And so you were
everything to me, that is now less than dust –
          lost, captive of the soil
That surrounds and nourishes my soul.

And so now I
still stranded, umbral shade of past passion –
          left, am guardian of sad recall
Watching branch and bloom hide memory's shrine.
Thus that soft lip which nourished me
With loving touch and kindly word
The loving gaze that held us all;
The hand which gently pressed.
So, the hair, the neck, the breast –
All these have been, and are now but ash
And phantoms lodged within my mind.

So Fate has left us
parted through life's cruel span –
          but, strong within mind's compass
is she held forever – Heft higher than the mason's stone.

Cottage Garden

Much more than half my life ago
Some chance led us to this place;
Now, my heart is caught and held
By the peace of its earth and space.

Some while past, when first she left me
I could not make my soul adjust
But cached it safe within the plot
Beside her memory and her mortal dust.

And as the family aged and spread
My lonely tenancy grew content
Past spectres guiding present life –
Perfect dreams too often dreamt.

So, time passes. Rooted, alone
This place is all I want or wish to know
And only where I wish to stay –
To tend, to minister, and bestow.

Where else would my heart worship?
The land, my chancel; the air my steeple cross
I am the warden, priest and choir
Cloistered with my earthly loss.

Alone

I am now more alone
That had so briefly gained
A joy of lifelong sharing,
A warmth of loving loved

I dream now more deeply
Where once I hoped to share
The joy of mutual peace
The peace of knowing known

I feel now a lesser self
Than that I might have paired:
The pain of prospects passing
To the realms of losing, lost

I mourn now the greater chance
That I so briefly saw
Better to have soared to crash, or
Sadder to have dreaming dreamed?

I know now that I have lost
All chance of hearthly peace;
Within a cloistered mind I see
My hermit cell planed lowly low

I am now more alone
That had the briefest chance
To love in coupled joy
The failed bond leaves crying cried

In the Veins of the Earth

What is that glint
        as the sod breaks and crumbles:
a sparkling hint
        of discovery
        as I dig the dusty summer soil?
This old garden has gained lost treasures
        of man, woman and child for centuries –
        What lies uncovered?

Teased from the clod
        I find a tiny glass heart and this symbol
breaks mine, for here
        is cached my soul
        with the mortal dust of all I ever loved.
In this plot her ashes lie at peace these many years
        yet now it sends a sign: weathered, soil-scuffed
        But still its facets shine

Leaning on my spade
        I rub it clean and buff it on my sleeve
tenderly, as if hers
        was restored to me
        each dusty face shines her passion.
Though time has passed and other memories fade
        I see her standing in her garden's sun
        As clearly as this heart

For many years we lived
      to love our cottage family home and plot
they passed too fast, and now
      I stay alone,
        sons grown to family fields anew.
But this earth's glass heart will hold my soul intact
      numen of her lovely presence here:
      My years now peaceful pass

Letters

Those love letters from the Seventies
I could not bear to read again
and could not bear to throw

Those airmail forms
those tortured lonely twelve-page laments
that I read and read so many times
in my cabin off Cape Town,
in Melbourne and Sydney:
So many words
So much love

But in the end
They were just ash
And I scattered them

Ashes to her ashes

Journeys

Retrospective

i

Innocent
      he met a force
Untried
          it held him

… and wonder drained the world of substance
          re-arranged the pages of his book to give more radiant a
                    reading.

The light of new possibilities
pressed down on time.
The girl sang to him 'You can hear the boats go by'. He   i
learned her mystery
     and destiny understood his loss.
She read 'Man is condemned to be free'. And he   ii
knew his responsibilities
     but flew with her wings

Newborn
… he spoke of peace and joy; saw the wonder
         of his destiny

and dreamed.
> The Daemons frowned on them
> and, remembering meaning,
> sought to divide   iii

... wiser, she saw another future; tasted their bitter gall
> but soared
> and vanquished all.

Time...
Peace came with distance. Fal smiled on them.
A lull
> when senses knew only a single silent bell
> He remembered
> 'Worship is transcendent wonder'   iv
and as they rose above the surf
> the gulls, and time itself, stilled: mute and 'mazed at
> > the clear karma of their love.
He devoured her mind; she drank his soul.
> The river becomes the sea
> > the tide welcomes its waters,
> > and it is content.

She drank at his well; was intoxicated by his spirit
> her gaze danced to his will
> his future was written in her eyes.
Later, the dark sands kept their secret:
> she wrote her love on his soul
> > he read her script and was lost

The night sea whispered

When you see such passion in her eyes
it's time to leave port
    the old sailor said

ii

Then
he became the high candle around which she flew
the tabernacle in which she dwelt:
    she was the centre of his being
    and all that he knew. The cedars whispered,
    the unicorns knelt and bowed their heads   v
    and Albina – she of the dawn, protector of ill-fated lovers –
    watched over them.
'Your body travels with me; your blood flows in my veins'
For the sway of his calling held him
    and on many days small partings disturbed them;
    briefly.
He did not leave her: only his body was absent awhile.
    She held his mind in thrall to her love

Life spun:
to the west the profane skills of the sea held him;
at each easting his very being was uplifted by her:
    she was his guru
    his sun.

It was as if eternity was theirs among the southern cedars

But even heaven knows a world beyond.
He knew.
He could only guess
      at her strength.
        For Llŷr called from the West, Eingana beckoned   vi
           He was a thing of the sea and parting was ordained:
              he must forever navigate old horizons
        She – for all her vision – could not see beyond the shore
He knows
the possibility of an orbit
      where umbral time is released by light
      long days on that higher plane eclipse longer darker time
      in earthly solitude
her body calls out for understanding
      and cries out…

He is torn
      but his odyssey is decreed:
      His ship awaits – the very seas wait to welcome him back.
      His earthly gods demand their due.

> The ghost of blind Teiresias prophesied, '… you
> ask about your sweet homecoming, but the god will
> make it a bitter journey. I think you will not escape
> Poseidon, the Earth Shaker, who is angered at heart
> against you… Even so, though you shall suffer, you
> and your friends may yet reach home… when you

> have escaped the dark blue sea… think only of your
> homeward course' ^{vii}

But Teiresias – for all his vision – could not see beyond the shore or
divine the suffering visited on this mortal man's Penelope.

iii

The night that has passed can never return:
    the sea quenches all.
Cruel parting after such passion
O woman left behind!

O ship
    Of steel, rivets: deck, bridge, hull and keel:
    Fore and aft, moored tight to her
    Cargo holds: soon filled
    Cabins! One cabin she knows so well!
Bearing him away

O man
    Of charts and night watches
    Scanning horizons: navigating so many seas
    Do you dream of her? Pine?
        Touch her in your dreams?

O woman left behind
    You can only pray…
    and wait:
        It is easier to sail away than be left at home!   viii

She could not hear his voice
Time stands still while his letters speak only from the past:
    write to the future and read of the past
    how do you talk when every penned sentence and its answer
    must crawl so far?
            you in me in you   ix
            they wrote

Memories!
Time is dammed in its hourglass: the stubborn sand
will not fall
she sees him drifting never nearer: a world away
    but she sees nothing!

    she cannot touch his body
    she cannot feel his soul
    she cannot sense his mind

On long southern seas beside the slow gliding albatross,
    it seems he too is burdened to drift these cold waters eternally;
time passes, but in passing still leaves its stubborn sands behind.
    Home has never seemed so far.
Without
    he sees her face in everything, at every turn
    her voice whispers

Calls.

Time passes.
And – because it is so ordained – once again
the great ship slides gently up her river
      the lovers are joined and… again… the cedars bow over them.

But then, but then
Must he, a sea-bound Sisyphus for ever reach with her the height
– so brief a crest – again to drift down in the spume
      to sea to crest sea's surge again, again; nor
      back to the pebbled shore
      beneath the pier?
Can either he or she withstand the tide's eternal wash?

iv

As to the watch a distant mast glint in the empty sea
As on the empty horizon an island speck appears
As in the night a breath touches his skin
So he became aware.
      the waves stretched out towards her and cirrus painted the way
      in his mind he held her
            her arms enfolded his being, her body welcomed and
            his late compass calmed their seas:
Their union had always been inevitable

And as again the land held him, she shared his joy…
the very land – each simplest sight: meadow, grove and stream
seemed dressed in brighter light   x
the flinty shore, the chalky downs sang with them
Old Ælle rejoiced   xi
Time and the world was theirs alone.
> The Daemons still frowned:
> sensing a different division,
> their power diminishing

Lace dressed she came to him
The waxy blooms she held seemed eternal
Her body is the ocean and every wave returns
> an echo of the vow. The churchyard trees hold the sound
> and the wind carries it forever:
> on its breath their love will always sing

They are alone!
> So short a time is left,
> her arms held him her body rejoiced she blessed his body
> his arms warmed her his eyes wept for her love
> he held her like a raft she held them afloat

So few days joined and they – who might then have then been rent
apart – saw a further heaven ope:
his lonely watch, her desolate vigil conjoined
to cross the seas companioned
> his lonely cabin cell now lighted, soul lifted
> his time now speeds – the sands not held

Above day's depthless deep unbounded sea
     and under many a star at night
she sees the distant blue the faint horizon round
the dolphin cleft wave at the bow the still albatross on station
sea-changing fog and mighty storms, Eingana's distant shores
     and understands their siren call

Tasting the sea brine, knowing the ship's noise
Swept by passing airs, dampened by blind fog
she travels
Stranger to the southern stars, guest of warmer seas
Lost to all she has known, hull cloistered
she travels
     By day, by night he keeps his watch
     and marks their time
     else, he wonders at their bounty, revels in their bliss
     embraces their time

But now his ship has voyaged too soon (would he had restrained its
                           course): one long year is ended
three departures and three homecomings mark the time
all things pass, her seat of learning calls
He cannot bear to leave

He knows she will struggle to write. Alone, he sees her weep
she yearns for his arms; her books no longer talk to her –
he is her text she reads his body repeatedly but
finds no sense. Alone, bereft,
she knows no shore

Where both had sailed, he sails alone. Adrift, his mind can only see
the currents of her sea: her body is his ocean
her mind his distant shore. He plots his course on her flesh
navigates his watch on her skin. He
is lost

When will he – pilot of the seas; helmsman of his destiny – return
his heart to homely Hestia's domain?   xii
        cross limen: see parlour, range and crib again?
        oceans crossed, is he securely docked within the cove, or
        can tide's ebb drag him hence?

Only the Moirai know   xiii

v

He will remember his summer homecoming:
The joy, the uncharted waters of surprise
The warm sun on the door, the bees in the honeysuckle.
She held him close and at arm's length, examined his smile
Understood his passion:
        he would never leave; the sea had let him go.

And now their life was compassed by a closer horizon
Hid from the old world, the larch watched over them.
Behind cattle sheds lost to sight

Walled with borrowed summer stone   xiv
      bounded by alder, beech and thorn
Their new haven held their hearts
      at ease:
no pilot would ease a seaward passage from this land
      this Elysian field where life is good to man

Ceredig's land became their home...   xv
Arianrhod seemed to smile on them: xvi
      And the home became fruitful
      Their time was blessed

Their home, the cottage, the old farm
surrounded them
      by day its land fed them
      at night its old roof creaked and rustled
        as if the mice were busy too

vi

Through tens of years their roots sank deep
Seasons passed...

Winter's bitter winds and Summer's softer edge
Strengthened their kinship with the land
The peace of its earth and space held them
its embrace enclosed them
      the only place they wished to know   xvii

But in that Spring
some tree, a field seemed somehow less
the hint of something passing
She read 'It is not now as it hath been of yore'   ^{xviii}
and he learned a new mystery
     and the Moirai knew his loss.

From that first love, that light which overcame the shades
     is left the warmth of memory
      These lines are legacy of
that heat which seared his mind and etched his soul
that love's dominion which held him
     worshipping

In the ashes of the fire there is a memory of the flame.

Notes

i   'Suzanne takes you down to her place near the river / You can hear
the boats go by / You can spend the night beside her' (Leonard
Cohen, 'Suzanne')

ii   'Man is condemned to be free; because once thrown into the
world, he is responsible for everything he does' (Sartre, *L'être et le
néant* [*Being and Nothingness*], 1943)

iii One derivation for the word 'daemon' is to divide

iv 'Worship is transcendent wonder; wonder for which there is now no
limit or measure; that is worship' (Thomas Carlyle lecture, 'The Hero
as Divinity')

v   The unicorn is the symbol of purity and grace. There are lines by W
H Auden, 'O Unicorn among the cedars / To whom no magic charm

can lead us' *(New Year Letter (January 1, 1940) To Elizabeth Mayer. Part Three).*

[vi]   Llŷr: Welsh god of the sea; Eingana: Australian aboriginal mother of all

[vii] Homer, *Odyssey*, Book XI: 90–149. Odysseus tells his tale: The Ghost of Teiresias. Translated by A S Kline. http://www.poetryintranslation.com/PITBR/Greek/Odyssey11.htm

[viii] 'Cruel Parting after Such Passion' (page 65), here quoted in full

[ix]   'I am in you and you in Me, mutual in Love Divine' (William Blake, *Jerusalem*)

[x]   Reference to William Wordsworth's 'Intimations of immortality' – here, the first shadow of the future

[xi]   Ælle: the First King of Sussex

[xii] Hestia: virgin goddess of the hearth

[xiii] Moirai: personification of fate – the Fates

[xiv] 'Summer (or hafod) stone': the walls are capped with stones from the library roof of the demolished stately home, Hafod

[xv]   Ceredig ap Cunedda (died 453), King of Ceredigion

[xvi] Arianrhod was the Celtic Goddess of fertility, rebirth and the weaving of cosmic time and fate.

[xvii] Echo from 'Cottage Garden' (page 88)

[xviii] Second reference to William Wordsworth's 'Intimations of immortality'

Water

MAN: In so short a time
   I saw a future
   Flow
   Created
   From the formless waters
   Born
   From the darkness
   The way begins
   All words are water
   Flowing

GAIA: From my innermost being
    I gave abundance!
   My words flow from the mountain top
   My words give succour to the land
   My words are the waters of the sea

PRIEST: The word was at the beginning
   and unto the end.

MAN: And behold
   I came from the sea
   Its words were my words

And the first of these was love.
The land welcomed me
The girl welcomed me
And she was my river
Words flowed from her depths
Onto my flesh

My eyes swam in her beauty
My mind spun in her eddies
My heart drowned.

O Pontus!
You have brought me here
O Gaia!
Bless our words

GAIA: Mortal man!
Words are ordained:
Worship the river that sustains you
Care for its waters
Welcome its wisdom

MAN: As a poet his words
As a tenor his aria
So my praise
Exalts this girl
    who brought me to the land

I worship her fluid form
    as I drift down
I praise her deepest depths
    as I sink below

PRIEST: Use the words with care!
Your God is the God of formless waters
riding with the seabirds
    swimming with the fish
        gathering in the clouds
Your prayers are heard by him
though they be dropped in the river's water
    as you swim over her pools
        or float on her currents
Your hymns are words of love
to the girl you hold above all else,
    praising her beauty as you see her
        worshipping her form as you hold her
But they are heard by him

GAIA: With Kybele
I rule the lands.
As you pass over me
As she runs through me
Blessings flow.
I shall remember
    the words.

GIRL: Kybele! Meter Oreia!
            Hear the waters flow.
            They sing of my joy:
                 As the ocean welcomes the stream
                 As the flood grows with my waters
                 He holds my very being

                 I delight in his currents
                             and take my pleasure in his oceans
                 We have become one!
                 As he holds me
                 Embraces
                 Loves
                 Me
                 Words
                 Flow loud
                 From my depths
                 And shoal in his waters!

MAN: United under one heaven
            The moon and stars and sun shine on us:
            Held together on the waves beneath the wind
            Held fast in worship.

                 She came to me that day
                      and as I held her, our joy poured
                      forth to calm
                      the winds

She came to me at night
    and as she held me, only the moon held sway:
    dawn was held at bay
She came to me by day
    and I held her close
And then it was as if
    that greater light which filled the sky
    flooded all earth with its radiant rule
And all the waters of the seas knew
    our passion and
    withdrew
    their dominion

GAIA: Welcome!
    As God has divided
    the waters from the earth
    So you are separated from the waters
        whose waves may yet crash around us
        whose floods may wash over us
    You are one with my land.
    As you have blessed it
        now its earth exalts you.

MAN: I hold
    Your promise
    You see
    Our future

rooted in the land
Your bounty
comes from its loam
We prosper!

PRIEST: Oremus!
All my words are water
Flowing
You have lived the way
Flowing
Your lives are water
Flowing
On our land

We receive you!

The Voyage

i

Callow, green, innocent!
    So you could describe him
    as he was delivered
    by his parents
        – fresh-faced and newly uniformed
    to his ship.

        They had made him wear it once before and,
        proudly watched him walk down the road, his
        first leather-soled shoes slippery on the paving.
        Then, as now, it felt heavy, too big, too new
        – wrong. His cap was enormous, the peak large
        and shiny and the white top ridiculously flat and
        wide. He has never before worn a shirt with a
        detachable collar (three of each purchased – as
        listed in the lengthy company list) and foresees
        trouble! He knows above all else it marked him
        out as new!

Huge against the busy dockside,
    moored by a tangle of ropes
    her gangway leading to a hole in her side –
    beyond that… just darkness,
she stands: his future!

The taxi had dropped them beside a steel-grey shed.
Between where they stood and where he guessed he needed to be
    were cranes and a bustle of hard-faced men
    all intent on lifting, carrying and heaving
Pallets of cargo swung through the air above them
    all was noise: shouting, whistles, crashes
    and the whine of motors.
      Small tractors rushed in with more cargo all the time
      before disappearing back into the shed behind them.
On board, more men could be seen waving at the crane drivers
    and then as the cargo swung over their heads
    rushing out of sight. Elsewhere, there is the spark of welding,
    men painting –
The activity is both wondrous and worrying!
    Perhaps he should understand what was happening!

The grey February London sky drizzles rain and – somehow – they
                       find their way to the gangway
    and are met by an important figure: the senior cadet
      rigidly polite to his parents, but impatient
      with this first-trip junior, marked out by his dress
      as hugely unknowing.

Eventually – parting over and with his father's unexplained aside:
    'If you can't be good, be careful'
    spinning in his mind –
He is left with his cases in the small L-shaped cabin he will share –
    and, as the junior, tidy, scrub, dust and polish –
    wondering what he should be doing!

Obviously he should unpack, but where is there
room for all his gear – he has sea boots and
oilskins as well as several types of uniform – and
only a small locker and a couple of drawers to
fill! … But what is expected of him? Should he
be somewhere else? Doing something else?
The unknown is almost terrifying!

It is three days before his cabin mates returned from leave.

ii

There is a week before they sail and most of it seems spent in limbo!
    Sent hither and thither on small tasks:
        carrying stores, polishing brass, covering hatches
        lowering flags, turning on lights
        a boat drill
    Sent ashore to collect the papers that will define his new life:
    assign him to the ship, let him cross seas.
Life seems full of empty time
He is lonely, writes letters home, reads.
    There is a group photo, a company inspection
His diary details every meal!

Every other cadet seems to know so much more
    even the nine who joined at the same time as he
    – these first-trippers: the 'Trippers'
He is told that he is Starboard Watch C

He is told that 'stations' are at two in the morning
      but is unsure what that means…
At two in the morning he discovers
      and spends two hours in the cold on the forecastle
      as they manoeuvre out of the Royal Albert Docks
            more or less without his help as he has no idea what to do
            He is either in the way or coiling the wrong rope

And so he is at sea, his first voyage begun.
Finally, on their second day at sea – already 500 miles from London
      the trippers are called together and told about their new life,
         at last he has some understanding of what is required.
Life begins to fall into a regular pattern.
              The day is divided into four: an hour before
              breakfast, morning, afternoon and early evening
              – the first of which will be either PT, seamanship
              or deck scrubbing. Watches are assigned to
              school, working below decks, or on deck or to
              one of the three bridge watches, where as juniors
              they either keep lookout, learn to steer or are on
              standby.
Days, dolphins and a small storm passed by
      days of chipping old paint, painting rails, scrubbing decks…
      a routine
      of sorts
He begins to feel as if he belongs –
      belongs at the very edge of this naval society
      belongs as if he had a place
      belongs to be tolerated until he is useful!

Too much time is left
        – he is unused to this need to organise his life for
                                                  himself –
  and fills it writing letters and a diary
                Each week his watch – Starboard C – is assigned
                one period each day in the school room to work
                on a correspondence course and learn the Rules
                of the Road at Sea. He struggles with spherical
                trigonometry, ship construction and ship
                stability, is slow to learn the 30 Rules by heart
                and is horrified at his failing to learn Morse
                code: reading out random letters and numbers
                in blocks of five as they are flashed from a tiny
                light near the ceiling by the 'schoolie' – a second
                officer.

And then there was the Canal.
      He still remembers it for his first sight and taste of watermelon
            the strange red flesh with its hidden black seeds
            never seen at home
            so refreshing
                in the sticky heat.
    and
    travelling so slowly there is little breeze –
    the heat is unrelenting.

He is off-duty and his diary records the day:
            the jungle so close on each side
            the convoy of ships held up at the huge locks

the little trains – the 'mules' – attached to the ship
    to hold her in position through the locks
the butterflies
the lakes
But more than anything else, the stately progress and the heat.

iii

Storms are chiefly memorable for the disruption to routine
    no early morning PT
    no work on deck
    cold meals
But his first Pacific storm –
    his first storm while on bridge watch – was different.
By some complicated algorithm
    watches are divided between hours on standby in the mess
    on the wheel and on lookout
Watches at night are called from their cabins
    by the standby of the previous watch:
        tonight he was first lookout.
    Knowing the weather, he prepares himself well:
        warm clothes and oilskins
    He is surprised to find the water-tight door to the foredeck
Closed
    but – with difficulty – undoes the dogs and forces it open
        against the wind
        staggers through and secures it again.
    His brain is telling him that this is ridiculous

as heavy spray crashes down
but there is a vague need to do what is expected of him
his duty –
and, hanging on to the safety lines put up during the day,
he staggers into the wind and spray
as the deck lurches and tips under him.

This can't be right!
What will it be like on the forecastle?
Quite scared he struggles on for six or eight steps
all his energy focused on the wire stretching forward

Suddenly
a spotlight hits him from the bridge
an amplified voice yells at him to get the hell back!
He fights his way back
through the spray
through heavy door
and reports to the bridge.

Here he is regarded as some kind of simpleton for venturing forward
there is scant sympathy from the Third Officer
his lack of knowledge about lookouts in bad weather
judged amazing!
Finally, late – in trouble again –
he relieves the lookout on the monkey island above the bridge!

Many years later, he will wonder how such poor
communication over such a vital matter of safety
could have happened. Why had nobody told

him? It will also become clear just how scared
the Third Officer must have been when he
spotted him on deck!

Then the Pacific becomes a mirror smooth blue
            with a long swell – the horizon is lost to the sky
      by day they see flying fish
      and find the occasional one on deck
      By night, lookout on the forecastle is magically amazing
            balmy breezes and millions of stars

… and a few days later, it is over
                        they arrive in Wellington.

Rooms

From an original idea by Conrad Aiken (1889–1973)

The Lounge

Netted windows with fawn roller blinds
lowered a little by their macramé tassels for his forty winks
Shush! Be quiet, he's having his nap, don't make a din –
or completely, when at night
he shovelled the last coal from the bin
concealed in its wooden cabinet
and lowered the heavy lid on the fire to keep it in

The Playroom

The old wind-up gramophone seemed to play
Forties tunes – 'Broadway Melody' and
'Drip, Drip, Drop Little April Shower' each day
when the Davy Crockett record smashed.
The tall 'black cupboard' stood by the door
with toys and a pile of *Marvel* comics
he brought back from the States in the war

The Dining Room

She waited for the key in the lock, the pause in the hall
and the loving, greeting kiss
and we began tea as he peeled and quartered an apple
carefully with his penknife
and she poured tea and passed cups

The School Room

>Of course there were old desks and huge radiators
>and a blackboard that rolled up its wisdom
>endlessly

The Garage

>No car – but a treasure-trove of old tools
>In a case, wireless valves and rheostats
>gave no hint of their use

The Workroom

>You bend the top of the wire into a hook and hold it
>beside the stem and twist it round
>or thrust it through a carnation from the stem
>make a hook and pull back down
>ready for another wreath or bride's bouquet
>repeat
>until the pots of blooms on the floor run out

A Bedroom

>Night-night, sleep well, you can read for ten minutes.
>Bureau closed on homework and the ink spill, not yet noticed,
>which ended the sad essay, 'What I did in the summer holidays'
>School clothes ready on the other bed

Lounge

>The piano fell into disuse
>His Für Elise had been as good as it got
>He never had the ear for it

A Cabin
>The loneliness of three bunks,
>three lockers, three lifejackets
>and a porthole

Another Lounge
>We watched *That Was the Week That Was*
>or Ken Russell's *The Music Lovers*
>and later with television in the background
>we were alone,
>the huge bay window curtained in velvet

Another Bedroom
>The bottom bunk bed was fine and not uncomfortable
>as I dreamed of her
>in the room opposite

Cabin 2
>Returning to his cabin after docking he found
>an open door and a uniformed man
>bending over his desk
>reading his letters:
>Little use in remonstrating –
>Hull was the home of UK Customs & Excise
>and now he felt sympathy with the crew
>who built false pipes in the engine room
>made from tins of Old Holborn tobacco

The Last Cabin

> She had known his cabin before.
> And now it was hers too:
> held between the thrum of the engines
> and the uneven sway of the sea
> she was unsure of her new life

The Bar

> Drinks before dinner
> Darts after dinner
> And anecdotes!
>> In return for some small jest
>> the Electrician pouring ink into the bath
>> of the 'Fridge Engineer –
>> Jim scrabbling his way out
>> as the black tide advanced.
> He's dead now – murdered in a Glasgow pub.

Saloon

> They stood politely for my wife
> as we arrived at the table
> for the first time
> and leaning forward as he sat again
> the Third Engineer's tie floated across his soup
> and broke the ice

A Kitchen

> When they arrived at the farm –
> daffodils poking through melting snow –

before they could ask about the cottage
she pulled them into the kitchen
with the tiny orphan lamb by the fire
and the kettle steaming on the stove
for a cup of tea

Their Bedroom

Kneeling on the bed
he looks down at her hair
spread on the pillow
in sleep

Seminar Room

The fusty fug of a small room
with too many students in it
seated on unmatched chairs
to discuss a Whitman poem
imperfectly understood

Office

Ten research papers explore
the use of psycholinguistics for...
Another dozen tell the way
software for simulating search may...

Cottage Kitchen

Old slate slab floor with old blue lino
old blue units with shelves collapsing
under the weight of china

Hospital Room

> An endless eternity ending
> The view over the town now strangely blurred
> A whispered word
> She never heard

His Bedroom

> Kneeling on the bed
> He sees stars
> in the perfect black
> above the shadow trees
> And hears an owl

ENDINGS

A series of 11 short poems

End of a Galaxy

A blink
In the silent depth of night

As the last leaf of the beech tree
     As the silent tear of my love

End of Harmony

I see her dancing on the sands

I see her   as she sees me
     and in that moment
     sand, sea, sun, surf
     vanish in the vortex
until
our love   born in the moment
     holds the world
     perfectly in place
until
the sands   will no longer hold her dance

End of a Journey

I was the ocean travelled

The sea was our book   she was its pen
Did she write of love on its pages
As her ink ran dry?

I do not know   we were one
     She was lost in my doldrums

End of the Name

Still it stays on the page hidden amongst the lines
I am the only one
who sees it

as every day   I hear
a silent song   raised
to our love
     these are mine alone

End of Dreams

Our flesh   melted
      in our flesh –
      you sing, I weep
      my tears are descant
      we are one

Our flesh   united
      in our love –
      you rose, I fell
      as the sea receded
      we were one

Between your soul and my soul
      life shone
      briefly

End of Love

Lovers lose the present   we hid the future
     in the years   We painted
     our life
     my hands were the shore
     her breasts the horizon

our flesh was the canvas and our blood the tempera

Every day her soul and her heart called us,
thrusting us forward, thrusting to the future:
we became
     rosebuds wilting in the desert sands

End of a Path

Where did the road begin
        our travels stretch out
        on our map?

Did I ink in that distant destination?

Now that the sands have covered her tracks

I wonder
Who did we meet
        make
        leave?

End of the Moon

Sylph, silver crescent of harvest
we dreamt in your arms

> dwelt in your spell:
> too long we loved

'The soft light will always
lead you to me' she whispered
and I entered her soul

> Night ends at your cleaving
> Sylph, sickle of lovers

End of Talk

He does not hear

words   sentences   whispers
          hearing hope
          I give none
          my body broken
                    in pain

somewhere in my years there are tears

still my blood pulses round
a last breath

End of Sanity

When the cold winds blew her soul from him
       he knew that death was a hollow laugh
       and love lay in her silent voice

In all the years he has stood naked
   on the shore:
      his morning
      his noon
      his night
      pressed cold against his flesh
         scourged by her dust

End of the Wind

The last specks of sand touched him
as the sun lit his face
raised to the horizon

later   his epiphany
    came in the lonely
        stillness
    of the dark night

Three Dreams in Tana

1: An Old Transformation

Her body
    cold
    as sea ice
lay before me
broken
    by life's swell.
I remembered
    the pull of her currents and tides,
    her surging waves and deeps
And I knew
I could no longer travel
the course
we had set
    so long before
As she lay before me
still, pale, cold
I wept:
            for ever
            becalmed

2: Lovers

Naked
she lay before me
as I looked down
seeing another flesh
remembering
that lost love
weeping for that old passion.

She held me in her arms
quietly
in that hotel room.

3: 24 Hours

In the dusk
she anointed me with love
In the night
she comforted my tears
In the dawn
she held my sorrow
In the day
she absolved my memories

Early Autumn Lake

Below the incurious sheep on the hill
    that stare at me as they endlessly chew
The sun is warm and I perch on a stone to watch quietly
As it is reflected off the surface of the lake:
    the part not covered with pond weed
        where flies dip and buzz
          dragonflies and damselflies dart
            and hover:
              red and blue liquid flashes
The sun stays warm on my back
A light breeze ripples the surface
    and rustles the taller rushes at the far end
But never a rise
    I think all the fish have been taken
There are the remains, a few feathers only,
    of a pheasant on the bank:
    an otter kill I think
The gamekeeper is on the island
    and I point out the remains
A duck takes off noisily as I walk on
    past the musical trickle of water
        falling from a culvert

Then
Everything is disturbed
    by a low military transport 'plane rumbling past

Again, silence settles on the surface

The Lounge

My rhymes form in clouds
over the armchair
beside my notebooks
and the fire

My lines are captured
and preserved
in the remains of the forest
immortalised on its pulp

My words are held captive awhile
in the bright prison cells
where machines etch their pain
on smooth white sheets

My once quiet thoughts crash
noisily onto the leaves
again and again
and are swept together

My open mind is close bound
and my couplets covered
held, forever ordered
dissonance forgotten

My captive codex is held
waiting in the dark
Later, I will be freed
into the world

… and in conclusion

Three Haiku

Where sea and sky meet
        a green flash from the set sun
Lighting distant shores

                In Spring my compass
                        navigated the world round
                Now Autumn tides ebb

In the Winter storms
        my old life invades the new
Waves crash past the strand